LOVIN' BLOOM

LOVIN' BLOOM

The Unauthorized Story of
ORLANDO BLOOM

Heather Kranenburg

BALLANTINE BOOKS • NEW YORK

A Ballantine Book
Published by The Random House Publishing Group

www.ballantinebooks.com

ISBN 0-345-47920-3

Manufactured in the United States of America

First Edition: June 2004

OPM   9   8   7   6   5   4   3   2   1

Contents

LOVIN' BLOOM

CHAPTER ONE

From Middle Class to Superstar

"I don't know any family that doesn't have a little story somewhere. Besides, if you didn't have those things in your life, you'd be so bland."

—Orlando in an interview for *GQ* magazine

Each year, more and more actors are introduced onto the Hollywood scene, grabbing the attention of the media and the hearts of millions of fans. But not all celebrities have that certain something that gives them staying power in the entertainment world, and it is rare nowadays to find the old Hollywood story of someone being "discovered," and plucked out of middle-class life to be turned into a star. But for *Lord of the Rings* star Orlando Bloom, this is exactly what happened. Orlando was not raised in a famous home, nor was he a childhood celebrity who made his way from television to the big screen.

It is Orlando's love of acting and his dedication to his roles that have put him on top today. He worked as hard as he could from when he was very young. Although his success on the big screen might have seemed sudden, it came only after much training and effort.

Fun Fact:
"Orlando" is of Germanic origin, meaning "One who is famous throughout the land."

In the beginning, Orlando was just an average boy in a small town who had a dream of being famous, but he had faith that if he worked hard at his goals, he could get what he wanted. His story begins on January 13th, 1977 in Canterbury, Kent, England, a small town an hour east of London. His father, Harry, named him after the Shakespeare character and seventeenth-century composer Orlando Gibbons. His mother later said that Orlando gained his name because Harry wanted something that would be easy to remember. Harry, an outspoken leader in the anti-apartheid movement, wrote books on his cause, and worked with the legendary leader Nelson Mandela. Because he had so many people following his cause, Harry often had many students, and he constantly confused their names—so he wanted a unique name for his son, one that everyone would remember easily. We don't know whether Harry suspected that by the time Orlando was in his early twenties, the whole world would know his name; regardless, the name has been branded onto the hearts of millions as Orlando's fans have watched him light up the screen over and over again.

Harry's strong opinions and outgoing personality greatly influenced Orlando. Sadly, he passed away when Orlando was just four years old. But when he was thirteen, Orlando found out that Harry was not his birth father. His real father was a family friend and his guardian, Colin Stone, who became the father figure in his life after Harry died. This news shocked Orlando, especially since he learned it

> **Fun Fact:**
> Orlando's hometown of Canterbury, Kent, is known for its famous cathedral and is the home of the University of Kent. Canterbury Cathedral, St. Augustine's Abbey and St. Martin's Church have been designated World Heritage sites in Canterbury. Millions of visitors travel to see them every year. The main cathedral is 557 feet high and is the center of the Anglican religion. Kent is known as "England's garden" because of its beautiful scenery and gorgeous flowers. Another site that many people visit when they are in Kent is Leeds Castle. Once a palace to King Henry VIII, it is now open to tourists all year.

at such a young age. However, he has said that he loves and respects both men as fathers and appreciates all they did for him while he was growing up. He says now that he was extremely lucky to have had two fathers, but that talking about them can be confusing. Orlando never knows whether he should say "my real father," "my birth father," or "my guardian" when describing each of the two men he has grown to know as his dad.

When he was a child, Orlando was much more creative than academic. He loved to be outside, and he loved sunny days in England. While he was in school, he must have daydreamed about all of the fun things he could be doing instead, like playing in the family's large house or in the garden. Often, his teachers would accuse him of being distracted, of staring out the window and not paying attention to what was being taught.

When he grew older, though, school interested him more. He studied photography and sculpture, and was very talented in both, achieving A-levels in art, sculpture, and photography. He then entered drama school, where he explored his creativity.

Orlando grew up in a loving and supporting home, and with his older sister Samantha around, he always had a companion to play with in the family's garden. His mother could never get the two children to come inside! They would stay in the garden for hours playing make-believe. They loved to pretend to be different characters, from pirates to soldiers. Even as a kid, he was into playacting!

From his sister, he also gained an interest in fashion from a young age. One of Samantha's favorite things to do with her little brother was to dress him up, and often she shopped at thrift stores for clothes for their dress-up games. Orlando had everything from loafers and preppy check shirts to cowboy boots and hats. So maybe that's why Orlando always wears the most interesting and up-to-date styles every time we see him!

Orlando has said that he is accident-prone, and has been since his childhood. An adventurous child, he was in and out of the hospital more times than he can count. As an infant, he cracked his skull. His mother was holding him outside, and when she bent over to pick up a stick of wood, his head smacked against a nearby tree trunk. Shortly after this, he was

> ### Cool Quotes:
> "I broke my leg when I was skiing and I had to wear a cast for a year. I sat at home really depressed . . . I was eating biscuits and chocolate bars. I was a porker."
> —Orlando on being accident-prone, *WHO* (Australia)

injured while crawling over a rock in the yard, and in another incident, a horse stepped on his foot! Orlando was just a baby who liked adventure and couldn't seem to stay out of harm's way. At eleven years old, Orlando broke his leg skiing. Later he broke his nose while playing rugby and his wrist while snowboarding. But his most dangerous accident would happen when he was older, after he moved to London.

Before that, when he was still living in Canterbury, and when he wasn't playing in the garden, breaking bones, or being dressed up by Samantha, Orlando was taking part in poetry- and Bible-reading competitions at the language school where his mother, Sonia, taught. His mother loved to teach, and was glad that her children wanted to take part in the activities that went on at her school.

One of the most exciting events of the year was the Kent Festival. Everyone in the town went and participated in many different activities. It was there that Orlando and his sister got their first taste of performing. They often participated in poetry readings, reciting poetry by Robert Frost. If you asked Orlando now, he would still be able to recite some of the poems from memory. He has said that his reading experiences at the Kent Festival inspired him to be an actor. They taught him how to speak in front of a crowd, and after his first few readings, Orlando did not have any stage fright. He loved performing for the people of Canterbury.

Orlando's education began at Saint Edmund's public school in Canterbury. His mother paid £9,000 (that's roughly $16,000 at today's exchange rate) a year to make sure that her son received the best education. It was there that Orlando first studied photography, sculpture, and theater. His theater teacher would often give

> **Fun Fact:**
> Orlando and his sister often won first prize at
> poetry-reciting competitions when they were children
> in Canterbury, Kent.

> **Fun Fact:**
> Orlando describes himself as "mildly dyslexic." Dyslexia
> is a learning disability that often results in a difficulty
> learning to read.

him interesting roles to try because he saw
Orlando's talent as an actor right away.

As a child, Orlando was interested in larger-
than-life characters, especially Superman. One
day, he found out that Superman wasn't real but
was actually a character played by an actor
named Christopher Reeve. Orlando decided
that the only way to become larger than life like
Superman was to become an actor and be a hero
on the big screen. When he was just nine years

old, Orlando had a girlfriend, and every day he and his friends would race to see who would become her boyfriend for the day. Orlando has said that he wanted to use Superman's great speed to reach her first. Maybe it was reaching the girls that really inspired him to become an actor!

Orlando has been quoted as saying that he got into acting because of the women. He has also said that as a child, community theater and acting in plays at school were important to him because he got to "hang out with the chicks."

The girls are definitely a plus, but Orlando is also very serious about his acting career. From the start, he has taken it seriously as a craft, and not just as a way to meet women. When he was only sixteen years old, he moved to London to act with the National Youth Theatre, the United Kingdom's premier youth arts organization. It was there that Orlando took courses in acting, stage management, lighting, and sound, as well as in costuming, scenery, and prop building. While he was in acting school, he made friends with an older crowd, and often went clubbing in London. He began to love the London nightlife. London was a bigger city than the small town of Canterbury, and he always found fun and new things to do there. He says that the school friends he made in London introduced him to many new life experiences, and his time spent at the National Youth Theatre was a period of great growth for him. It was also during this time that he landed a role in the British television series *Casualty*. It was not a large role, but it gave Orlando experience working in front of the camera. His talent and dedication landed him a scholarship with the British American Drama Academy, where he continued his education in theater and the arts.

Fun Fact:

At age thirteen, Orlando got his first job, as clay trapper at a shooting range. A clay trapper loads and aims the clay discs used as targets in the shoot. Clay discs replaced live pigeons as the preferred target in the nineteenth century.

During one term with the Academy, Orlando played the lead role in the play *A Walk in the Vienna Woods*. Orlando's talent was finally being recognized, and he decided to hire an agent. This led to roles in British television and eventually to being cast in the film *Wilde* in 1997.

Considered to be Orlando's big break, *Wilde* is the life story of playwright and critic Oscar Wilde. It was in this film that Orlando worked with fellow British actor Jude Law. Orlando played a rent boy, and although his part had only one line, he made an impression in the role. After the movie was released, Orlando was flooded with offers of roles in movies and television, but instead of jumping at these chances, he decided to further his education at the Guildhall School of Music and Drama. He wanted more room to be creative, and studying at Guildhall would give him this opportunity. Ewan McGregor also attended Guildhall, before Orlando got there. Orlando looked up to Ewan and saw his headshot in the hall as one of several well-known graduates. As he looked at the photo, he must have dreamed that one day he, too, would be famous.

At Guildhall, Orlando was very active in his theater studies and he performed in a variety of plays such as *Little Me*, *A Month in the City*, *Peer Gynt*, *Mephisto*, *Twelfth Night*, *The Trojan Women*, *The Seagull*, *Three Sisters*, *The Recruiting Officer*, *Antigone*, *Uncle Vanya*, *A*

Fun Fact:
Orlando has broken his ribs, his nose, his legs, his back, his arm, and his wrist.

Night Out, and *Mystery Plays*. He also made guest appearances on two British television shows, *The Ben Elton Show* and *Misnomer Numbers*.

Things were looking up for Orlando. His performances at Guildhall were spectacular, winning praise from teachers and audiences, and his television appearances were opening more and more doors. But just as everything was going perfectly, tragedy struck. In 1998, while trying to climb onto a rooftop terrace, the pipe he was climbing tore away from the building. Orlando slipped and fell three stories. That's just the type of person Orlando was and always will be: a bit of a daredevil. The pipe was there and in the spur of the moment he thought it would be cool if he climbed it—and it was, until things went wrong. He was rushed to the emergency room of a nearby hospital, where doctors told him that he had broken his back. Doctors said that his chances of ever walking again were slim to none. In an instant, Orlando saw all of his hopes and dreams disappear. He must have thought his career was over. Doctors bolted metal plates to Orlando's spine to stabilize it and help it heal properly. Then Orlando underwent intensive rehabilitation to learn to walk again. With careful supervision and treatment, Orlando miraculously walked out of the hospital on crutches only twelve days after the accident.

Once out of the hospital, though, Orlando had to take medicine for the pain he was suffering. He also had to wear a back brace for a year after the surgery. Like many teenagers, Orlando jumped ledges and never thought about the consequences; he probably never imagined he would get hurt. Now, he has a new appreciation for life. He has said that his back is a constant reminder of how lucky he really is. He knows now that he is not unstoppable and that there are dangers out there. The accident also made Orlando aware of how many people care about him. Now, he says that he takes the time to tell the people he cares about that he loves them and doesn't take one moment of his life for granted.

COOL QUOTES:

"The doctors said I wouldn't walk at all. I chose not to believe them. I thought, that's not me, that's somebody else."

—Orlando's reaction to his injury, *GQ*

He continued to study at Guildhall while he recovered, and just two days before his graduation, he was informed that he was going to be cast as Legolas in the trilogy of films based on J.R.R. Tolkien's *Lord of the Rings,* with Peter Jackson directing. Peter Jackson actually came to Orlando's school to tell him in person, and Orlando was so excited that he wanted to run through the halls! Orlando had sent in an audition tape, hoping to be considered for the part of Faramir. When the casting directors saw the tape, though, they knew that he would be perfect for the role of Legolas, which is a much larger role than that of Faramir. Orlando did not try out for this role because he figured he was too inexperienced for it. He was wrong! Even though the casting directors had only seen a short audition tape, they knew they had found a star. Orlando was to be the elf prince of Mirkwood, and was set to leave for New Zealand to begin filming right after his graduation from Guildhall. As he was about to finish drama school, he had a budding career in the entertainment world, but how big was his career going to be? Only time would tell what was in store for Orlando, and as he anxiously packed his bags and boarded the plane for New Zealand, he knew he would have a whole new life ahead of him by the time he returned.

CHAPTER TWO

From Educated to Elvish: Orlando Makes It to the Big Screen

> "I got to dress up in funny clothes and run around New Zealand with a bow and arrow for eighteen months, how bad could that be?"
>
> —Orlando Bloom on playing Legolas,
> *i–D* magazine, December 2001

Orlando Bloom may have been the biggest discovery from the *Lord of the Rings* films. For any of you who have seen Orlando Bloom as Legolas in the *Lord of the Rings* trilogy, he looks quite different from the sleek, handsome heartthrob who often appears at film premieres and Hollywood events wearing a gorgeous suit and with his curly brown hair carefully tousled. To transform himself into Legolas, the warrior elf prince of Mirkwood, Orlando wore a long blond wig, makeup, blue contacts—and we can't forget the pointy ears! As soon as he graduated from Guildhall in 1999, he left for New Zealand to begin eighteen months of filming with fellow talented actors Sir Ian McKellen, Sir Ian Holm, Liv Tyler, Elijah Wood, and Cate Blanchett. For their roles, each actor had to become well acquainted with the works of Tolkien, and before the film began the actors talked about *The Lord of the Rings* in depth. Often, the cast would get together during their free time to talk about their acting and the story line of the movie. Hearing each other's interpretations of the work often helped them play their parts better and make the scenes more realistic. When Orlando first met Liv Tyler, they played pool while discussing their roles. Tolkien's epic trilogy had to become their Bible if they were going to play their roles well. All of the actors in

---

COOL QUOTES:

"Elves are cool, man."

—Orlando on playing Legolas,
The Sunday Times (UK), December 2003

---

the movie say they now feel like experts on the *Lord of the Rings* books.

Before being cast as Legolas, Orlando was not very familiar with the *Lord of the Rings* books. He likes to read, and first started to read the books when he was fourteen years old, but he admitted that he put them down without finishing them. He could never find enough time for them between all of his adventures! But now that he has done the movies, the *Lord of the Rings* books are his favorites, and he has said that he now gives them to friends as gifts because he loves them so much.

New Zealand, where the movies were filmed, is an island nation in the South Pacific Ocean right near Australia. The films were shot near the capital city, Wellington, which has become a large tourist city over the past few years. Known for its culture, art, music, and restaurants, the city is a small urban area divided into six different districts, each of which has its own style and theme. Each district had many things to offer the cast and crew during their time off from filming.

Orlando took advantage of all the city had to offer. He and his fellow cast-mates often ate in Wellington's many great restaurants, such as the Chameleon Restaurant and Bar, or the Sakura Restaurant, known for its great Japanese food. They also attended plays in Wellington's theater district.

Orlando also learned how to surf on Wellington's south coast. The waves are so big, he was probably scared at first, but in true Orlando style he jumped right in and enjoyed the challenge. Now, Orlando loves to surf and does it whenever he can.

Often he would go to the coast to take a break from filming or to watch the seals, which were always hanging out on the beaches or on rocks in the water. One time, though, a seal caught him and his friends by surprise. They were in the surf when they saw a dark shape. They thought it was a shark! When they found out that it was really a seal, they all thought it was hilarious, but not Orlando. He is afraid of sharks and he got out of the water immediately. No matter how much his friends tried to convince him to get back in, he wouldn't go swimming or surfing for the rest of the day!

The scenery of New Zealand is gorgeous, filled with tall mountains, green pastures, and sunny coasts, so there was always something to do or see. Orlando has said that if he could revisit one place from the locations where he has filmed, he would choose New Zealand. The beautiful forests and dramatic shores make you feel like you are in another world.

One of the things that make the *Lord of the Rings* film trilogy so amazing is the special effects. When Orlando arrived in New Zealand, one of the first things he wanted to do was go to the special effects studio to see what was in store for him. When he got there he was in awe because of the rows and rows of costumes and armor. The studio had everything from bows and arrows to wigs to all of the elf costumes Orlando would be wearing during the movies. It was then that he realized just how large and involved the task of filming *The Lord of the*

Rings would be. Speaking of costumes, Orlando had three different blond wigs that he wore for the part of Legolas, each of which was worth at least $5,000. That's a lot of money for fake hair! He spent hours in costume and makeup each day before he filmed. Orlando always hated the makeup and costuming process because he often had to be there early in the morning and it took forever; the pointy ears that he had to wear took two hours to put on.

He often wanted to wear his elf ears out to the bars and clubs in New Zealand as a joke, but because the filming of the movies was so secretive, Orlando was not allowed to show them to anyone outside of the cast and crew. Orlando did give his girlfriend at the time a good laugh, though. One night, he was going back to his room for a quick nap between scenes, and he forgot to take his ears off. When he went to hug his girlfriend, she put her hand on his head and felt not the ears that she was used to, but instead, two giant pointy ears poking her!

Since this was Orlando's first big role, he must

have been very nervous. He was working with talented, experienced actors who were well acquainted with how movies worked. In order to get a sense of what being in movies was all about, he watched how the other actors were going about what they were doing. It was yet another learning experience for Orlando, and he took tips from all of the actors in order to put on a good show himself. He has said that filming *The Lord of the Rings* was like a continuation of school for him. He learned so much from everyone about how to act in front of cameras in a big-time movie production.

Orlando had reason to feel more confident because his role did not have a lot of lines to learn. His one problem with some of the scenes was his costume. Sometimes the heavy blond wig he was wearing would get caught in his bow and arrows and come right off his head! Then the makeup and costume crew would have to fix him up immediately so that he could go right back to filming.

Legolas Greenleaf, Orlando's character, is

2,931 years old and is an expert at fighting evil. Legolas became a member of the

---

COOL QUOTES:

"I have a great job. I get to dress up and become somebody else, especially when it's someone like Legolas, who's this super-cool kind of otherworldly elf. It's, like, I'm lucky, man, so why would I not appreciate that?"
—Orlando on playing Legolas,
Dolly magazine (Australia), 2002

Fellowship of the Ring after vowing to protect Frodo (played by fellow hottie Elijah Wood) in his quest. Legolas is known for the power of his strong and precise bow and arrow. Throughout the trilogy, he is the eyes and ears of a nine-member fellowship as they make their long journey through Middle Earth to destroy a ring filled with evil that the Dark Lord Sauron is trying to recover. Being an elf, Legolas is immortal. He can only be killed in battle or if his heart is broken (aww, even elves are romantic).

Elves are known for being very quick on

their feet and graceful. They also have excellent hearing and Legolas has several scenes in the movie where his hearing is a vital tool in tracking the enemy.

Legolas may not be Superman, but it was through this character that Orlando finally got to play the larger-than-life image he dreamed of as a child. Being larger than life is not an easy job, though! Legolas was a very difficult role to play because it involved many action sequences. Before filming began, Orlando had to become a master at archery, horseback riding, and swordsmanship. He says now that he knows how to do all of these things and although they are not particularly useful in today's world, in the past these skills would have made him a hero.

The first day he arrived in New Zealand, the directors put a bow in his hands so he would become familiar with it and look natural while holding it. He also studied Akira Kurosawa's *The Seven Samurai*. By the end of his training he became so skilled in shooting that he was using his bow and arrow to hit paper plates that trainers would throw into the air.

Though Legolas does not have many lines in the *Lord of the Rings* films, his quick and precise actions make his character the most memorable in them. Through training, Orlando developed fighting styles that became unique to his character. Orlando feels that playing Legolas has helped him to become more coordinated and balanced because of his character's focus and grace. He hopes that he took pieces of Legolas with him after he was done filming. Before this role, Orlando may have thought of himself as very clumsy, but he doesn't think so now. If you thought that elves were those funny, short, unlovable brown creatures, you were wrong! Orlando is definitely the hottest elf ever to grace the screen.

Along with learning what it takes to perform the stunts in the *Lord of the Rings* films, Orlando had to learn the language of Elvish, which J.R.R. Tolkien created specifically for *The Lord of the Rings*. It's a very hard language

> **COOL QUOTES:**
> "I think that came from the *Lord of the Rings* DVD where I was jumping out of airplanes and doing bungee jumps. New Zealand is a real outdoor sports place, I don't go around looking for bungee jumps!"
> —On his reputation as an adrenaline junkie,
> BBC interview, 2003

to speak, and is based on a Celtic dialect mixed with Old English. On Orlando's first day, he seemed quite embarrassed when he could not say the Elvish lines perfectly. The directors laughed and reassured him that speaking Elvish is like learning an actual new language—it takes time and unfortunately it's just not as useful! But, just like everything else, with some practice Orlando picked up the language and made it his own, adding to the character of Legolas and making Tolkien's work come alive on screen.

Although some actors would be very upset about spending a year and a half away from home, Orlando loved it! While in New

Zealand, he took advantage of all the beautiful country had to offer. He has referred to himself as an adrenaline junkie in interviews, and his time in New Zealand was no exception. He tried bungee jumping and surfing for the first time, as well as white-water rafting, skydiving and snowboarding. Despite his once-injured back and notorious history of injuries, Orlando became known as the daredevil of the cast.

While the cast couldn't wait to hear what new adventures Orlando took part in each day, the producers constantly warned him not to do anything that would lead to injury because they could not waste any time in the filming. If Orlando got hurt, they would have to delay taping any scenes featuring Legolas, and it would waste a lot of production time. Orlando assured the crew that he would be extremely careful, but in typical Orlando fashion, he managed to injure himself anyway, not with extreme sports, but while filming a scene. While shooting on horseback, Orlando's horse

fell, trapping him and cracking his rib. This
didn't stop Orlando, though. He was back
filming again only two days after it happened.
As for the horse, well, he was fine, just a little
shaken up by the fall.

* * *

Because all three *Lord of the Rings* movies
were shot in a single eighteen-month period,
filming was often confusing. Orlando would
sometimes have to be reminded of what had
happened in the script right before the scene he
was shooting, because they did not film the
scenes or even the movies in order. The cast
might have to do a scene from the third movie
in the morning, then a scene from the first in
the afternoon. This was a better way of filming
because everything got done much faster, but it
was still confusing to the actors, who had to
learn the whole trilogy in a very short time
period.

Orlando holds a special place for the *Lord of*

Surfing Terms Orlando
and His Cast-Mates May Have Used:

Air: Open air between a surfer, his board, and a wave—like when a skateboarder soars off a ramp and "catches air"!

Barrel: Also a "tube." The hollow part under the top of a wave

Carving: Like a knife, a surfer cuts across or "carries" the surface of a wave

Fin: Used to help balance a surfboard, the wedge of plastic that hangs below the board. Some boards have more than one

Hang Ten: Classic surfing term. A surfer rides his board with both feet squarely placed on the tip of the board

Leash: Rope that attaches the board to your ankle

Nose: The front of the surfboard

Stick: A board

Wipe-out: To fall off your board

the Rings films because of the friendships that he made while on set. After filming and spending so much time together, the *Lord of the Rings* cast became a family, and they shared many memorable experiences while in New Zealand. Viggo Mortensen, who plays the character of Aragorn in the film and appears in many scenes with Orlando, formed a very close friendship with Orlando. The two often went fishing, surfing, or out into the city of Wellington together, and they teased each other endlessly. Viggo would often call Orlando "Elf-boy" and Orlando would call him "Filthy human," because of the characters they play. When Viggo would tease him and tell him that elves are prissy and they are too worried about their appearance, Orlando would respond with "Elves live forever, you hear that! FOREVER!" Despite their on-screen differences, off screen the two formed a friendship that they still have today.

Filming *The Lord of the Rings* was a memorable experience not only for Orlando, but for all of the actors. They were so influenced by the time that they spent together that they

---

ONE OF ORLANDO'S FAVORITE SCENES:

Orlando recalls taping a scene where he is supposed to be swinging off the back of an elephant. It was one of his favorites to shoot. The elephant was built out of sandbags, and Orlando was wired and rigged to climb it with arrows and swing onto it as if it was a real elephant. He alternated climbing the bags himself and letting a stuntman do it, but he had to tell the stuntman exactly what to do so that it would look as if Legolas was climbing.

COOL QUOTES:

"I'm quite specific about what I want to ink myself with because they're there forever."

—Orlando, on his tattoo,

Dolly magazine (Australia), 2003

decided to get something to remember their experience forever—tattoos! After much discussion and convincing, the nine actors who were part of the "fellowship" in the film agreed to get matching symbols. Well, almost all nine—one of the members had his stunt double get the tattoo in his place. The tattoo is the Elvish symbol for nine, and Orlando has his on his forearm.

Although the actors made a pact not to let the tattoos be seen by the public, some of the cast members have shown them from time to time on talk shows or during interviews. Orlando kept his promise to his cast-mates, but if you look closely at some of his scenes from *Pirates of the Caribbean,* you can see the small symbol on his forearm. In addition to his tattoo, Orlando wears a ring with the Elvish saying "To wherever it may lead" engraved on it. It was given to him by one of the makeup artists on the set. There was big news in the tabloids when Orlando wore the ring from the movie on his left ring finger. People thought he had gotten married while filming! Orlando cleared up these rumors though, and usually wears his ring on his middle finger now.

The first *Lord of the Rings* movie, *The Fellowship of the Ring,* was released in December 2001, and audiences went crazy for it. It was an instant box office hit as well as one of the highest-grossing movies of all time. But the question asked by almost everyone who saw the film was "Who is that blond-haired elf?" Instantly, Orlando was thrown into the spotlight, and actors and audiences were amazed by his great looks and even better acting skills. Out of nowhere, Orlando's face was appearing everywhere from billboards to magazines to Internet sites. It was hard to believe. Just two years before the filming he was still in drama school. Now, he had action figures in every toy and collectible store that resembled his face; fans were screaming his name from the sidelines of premieres; and his personal life was becoming public to every *Lord of the Rings* fan, not to mention every teenage girl.

Everyone seemed to want to know every detail about this new star. Out of nowhere, Orlando went from being an inexperienced student to being handed a new life, a new career, and thousands of people who wanted him, or wanted to be him.

And of course, you can't forget the awards! Orlando won Best Breakthrough Male at the MTV movie awards in 2002 with *The Fellowship of the Ring,* which also took the Best Movie award. He was also nominated with the rest of the cast for Outstanding Performance by a Cast at the Screen Actors Guild awards. Orlando also won Best Debut at the 2002 Empire awards and Best Newcomer in *SFX Magazine*'s Top 10 Sexiest Men Awards. He was also named one of *Teen People*'s 25 Hottest Stars Under 25. At the 2002 Academy Awards, *The Fellowship of the Ring* was nominated in thirteen categories: Best Picture, Best Makeup, Best Visual Effects, Best Original Score, Best Original Song, Best Sound, Best Cinematography, Best Art

Direction, Best Screenplay Based on Material Previously Produced or Published, Best Director, Best Costume Design, Best Editing, and Best Supporting Actor. It took home the awards for best cinematography, best original score, best makeup, and best visual effects. The fan letters came pouring in, the movie was a success, and Orlando was in shock. Who would have thought that he would be this lucky, especially in his first big role! Most stars

Fun Fact:
Orlando was named one of *E! Online*'s Sizzlin' Sixteen Stars of 2002 after his breakout success in *The Fellowship of the Ring*.

have to wait years and go through many failures before finally having their careers take off.

And the audiences wanted more! They anxiously waited for the second *Lord of the Rings* film to be released. *The Two Towers* picks up right where *The Fellowship of the Ring* leaves off. At the beginning of this movie, we find Legolas trying to find the kidnapped hobbits, Merry and Pippin, but he ends up getting caught in a battle to save a race of humans that are going to be destroyed by the Uruk-hai army. With three different storylines going on at once, the movie is much more fast-paced than *The Fellowship of the Ring*.

Of course, most sequels never live up to the first film. But was this true for *The Two Towers*? No way! Again, the *Lord of the Rings* film was a huge success. What was the best thing about the movie? More Legolas! Orlando won the 2003 AOL Moviegoers Award for Best Supporting Actor and was named Best Actor of 2003 in *Rolling Stone* magazine. The cast was again nominated for Outstanding Performance by a Cast at the Screen Actors Guild Awards and *The Two Towers* was named Orange Film of the Year at the 2003 BAFTA awards. It also won another Academy Award nomination for Best Picture.

With the success of the first two *Lord of the*

Rings movies, everyone was anxious to see what the third would be like. The cast did it again. The last movie in the trilogy, *The Return of the King,* sold out at box offices everywhere and left fans wishing that the movie trilogy would never end. The film had everything: drama, romance, self-sacrifice, friendship, and even a little bit of comedy. And again, awards, awards and more awards! *The Return of the King* was the king of the Academy Awards in 2004, winning Best Art Direction, Best Makeup, Best Costume Design, Best Visual Effects, Best Director, Best Film Editing, Best Sound Mixing, Best Writing (Adapted Screenplay), Best Original Score, Best Original Song, and—finally—the coveted Oscar for Best Picture. The film also won four Golden Globe Awards in 2004.

The Return of the King pulled in the second-highest box office gross of all time, an amazing $1.1 billion. As the film's success sky-rocketed, so did Orlando's fame, success—and not to mention salary! Here

Orlando was, in his mid-twenties, a wealthy Hollywood superstar.

But, to go back to January of 2001, when the *Lord of the Rings* trilogy had just finished taping, Orlando, after a year and a half of working in front of the cameras in New Zealand, was ready to take on more films. First he retreated to his home in London for a little relaxation—eighteen months of filming can really make you tired! Then he decided to move to Los Angeles to start a serious film career. As offers came pouring in for Orlando, he had to sit down and make choices about the direction he wanted to go in the film business. He was serious about his career, but he had no idea what was in store for him, and must have wondered how he would choose the right roles. Little did he know he would again get to dress up and prepare himself for more action in movies that could boost his career even higher than *The Lord of the Rings*!

LOVIN' BLOOM

> **Sad Fact:**
> Because of his move to Los Angeles and the constant travel of his new film career, Orlando had give away his beloved dog, Maud. A family friend adopted the pooch.

CHAPTER THREE

Orlando in the Spotlight

> "I've been an elf, a soldier boy, a boxer, a pirate, and an
> outlaw. I really am every living boy's dream."
> —Orlando on his sudden rise to fame,
> *HQ* (Australia), 2003

BLACK HAWK DOWN

After finishing the filming of *The Lord of the Rings,* Orlando landed a role in the much anticipated movie *Black Hawk Down,* to be directed by Ridley Scott. *Black Hawk Down* is about an elite group of U.S. Army Rangers and Delta Force soldiers sent to Somalia on a mission to capture a warlord. What should have been a simple search-and-capture operation lasting under an hour turned into a hellish fifteen-hour-long battle. When the troops were finally evacuated, eighteen soldiers were dead and many

43

more wounded. In the film, Orlando plays an American soldier who breaks his back—a situation with which Orlando had had personal experience. His character falls seventy feet, and his injuries force him to stop fighting.

Fans also got to hear Orlando do something he hasn't done before—speak with an American accent. His role was small in *Black Hawk Down*, but he received great reviews for his performance and was becoming more and more of a household name. Orlando liked dressing up to play a soldier, and again did his stunts without the help of a stuntman.

Fun Fact:
For *Black Hawk Down*, Orlando had to learn an American accent.

Fun Fact:
Although *Black Hawk Down* was filmed after *The Lord of the Rings: The Fellowship of the Ring*, it was released in the theaters before *LOTR*.

NED KELLY

After *Black Hawk Down,* Orlando was cast to play the part of Joe Byrne in the Australian film *Ned Kelly.* Using Robert Drew's book *Our Sunshine* as its basis, the film focuses on the Kelly Gang and its crime spree from 1878–1880. Kelly (played by Heath Ledger) steals from the rich to give to the poor, just like Robin Hood. Opinion is divided about Kelly's history, though: Many Australians view him as a victim of the police and a national hero for rebelling against the law, but others believe that he was a merciless killer who deserved to be punished for his crimes.

Orlando's character, Joe Byrne, is a ladies' man with looks to kill. Girls swoon when they meet him, overwhelmed by his charming nature and striking appearance. Orlando's look for this movie is much different from that of the well-groomed, blond Legolas. Byrne is an unshaven Irishman, more rough than smooth. But Orlando did get to play around with his speaking voice again in *Ned Kelly*, adopting an Irish brogue. He loved the accent so much that he continued speaking with it when he wasn't filming. He went out to bars, restaurants, and pubs and kept the accent the whole time!

The character Joe Byrne is an unlikely criminal. He is the oldest son of farmers, a quiet, good-looking, well-educated and well-spoken man. His family has money and power, so he doesn't need to steal. He is the brains behind the gang: Ned Kelly runs the show, but Joe Byrne is the one who plans what the gang is going to do next. He is a dark character who drinks, does drugs, and goes against the law, often without shame or regret. In the end, out of desperation, he turns his gun on his friend. Orlando's wild side helped him to play the gang member. He channeled his energy and adventurous nature into the character.

The Kelly Gang's long and dangerous crime spree ends with a legendary showdown outside the notorious Glenrowan Inn, where the gang battled over one hundred armed policemen.

During the scene, the actors were fired at with metal pellets so that they could experience what the real Kelly Gang had. The pellets didn't hurt much, but the cast wasn't expecting them and many reacted with shock, giving the director just the expressions he wanted for the film. What a surprise for the actors, though!

The movie is based on a true story, and the real Joe Byrne died when he was only twenty-one years old. Orlando said that sometimes he felt like he couldn't sleep at night, or he would get scared thinking that the real characters were going to haunt him.

Orlando was also known as the matchmaker of the set. He hooked up fellow cast-mates Heath Ledger and Naomi Watts. He went to nightclubs with Naomi knowing that Heath would be there, then left the two of them alone together.

Ned Kelly was released in Australia on March 27, 2003 and got great reviews from audiences and critics. Orlando was once again praised for his wonderful acting. The film had the third-largest opening day box office sales in

Australian history, and hit theaters in the United States in 2004.

Fun Fact:
When first asked, Orlando did not want to play the role of Jimmy Connelly, and took the part as a favor to a friend. But once he did the role he loved it.

THE CALCIUM KID

After *Ned Kelly,* Orlando was cast in the film *The Calcium Kid* as a British milkman, Jimmy Connelly, who becomes a boxer. The film would be shot in London, which Orlando was excited about because he missed his home, family, and friends after so many months of filming all over the world. He had to train every day for his new part. He did not need to be big and bulky, just muscular and toned, and, although his character drinks a lot of milk, Orlando was told to avoid dairy as well as other fattening foods while preparing for his role. The movie was filmed on a very low budget—just a little over a million dollars. The whole movie cost less to make than the price of the after-party for the *Lord of the Rings* movies!

In *The Calcium Kid,* Jimmy Connelly loves his job as a milkman and dreams of becoming the regional manager of Express Milk Dairies. He has two close friends, Stan and Herbie Bush, with whom he spends much of his time. He enjoys boxing as a hobby, but when Herbie, who manages a gym, needs an emergency replacement for an ill boxer, he agrees to try it professionally. Herbie thinks that because Jimmy drinks so much milk every day, his bones and teeth will be strong enough to endure a fight. The only problem is that Jimmy has never been in a real boxing match before, and he's fighting a champion boxer defending his title.

> **Fun Fact:**
> Although he plays a milkman, Orlando prefers soy to dairy, and he is also a vegetarian.

Jimmy is charming, honest, and innocent, but he is also a bit of a geek. Orlando has said that he was excited to play someone who wasn't self-assured and cool for a change. Jimmy does not want to let anyone down, especially his father, and this allows him to be manipulated by everyone around him, including Herbie and Stan. Jimmy trains very hard for the short week that he has to prepare to fight the world champion, Jose Mendez. He is nervous and anxious, and knows that he doesn't stand a chance, but he has to give it his best and prove that he did all that he could to train and prepare. In the end, Jimmy becomes the hero of the fight and all of his dreams come true.

During the filming of *The Calcium Kid,* Orlando became good friends with actress Billie Piper, and the two chatted nonstop between takes. But don't worry, girls, Billie is married! Although the film's actors are largely unknown in Hollywood, Orlando has said that he worked with a magnificent cast on *The Calcium Kid* and that he loved filming it. The film was released in

England in April 2004 and was a big hit among teens in particular. A release date for the United States has not yet been set.

COOL QUOTES:

"Will is very eager and dependable. He's a blacksmith by trade and a master swordsman. He's a man of honor, in a time when, really, there is no honor—the polar opposite of Jack Sparrow. Will would throw his cape over a puddle for a woman. The character has a great arc; as he develops you see that he learns the way of the pirate."

—Orlando on Will Turner,
his character in *Pirates of the Caribbean*,
Disney magazine, 2003

PIRATES OF THE CARIBBEAN

Following the media hype surrounding *The Lord of the Rings*, Orlando was cast to play Will Turner in the Disney movie *Pirates of the Caribbean: The Curse of the Black Pearl*, in which he stars alongside the talented Johnny Depp. Orlando was very excited to be working with Johnny, who was one of his Hollywood idols.

> **Fun Fact:**
> Johnny Depp was first made famous by his role in the 1980s television show *21 Jump Street*.

The movie is based on a ride in Disney World, Pirates of the Caribbean, and if you have been on the ride, you will notice some familiar parts from it portrayed in the movie. Though Orlando has never been on the ride, he does a great job playing a nobleman and a pirate.

Pirates of the Caribbean was filmed from October 2002 to February 2003, partly in Burbank, California at the Disney studios.

> **Fun Fact:**
> Walt Disney came up with the idea for the Pirates of the Caribbean ride at Disney World himself.

Disney had sets such as the hold of a pirate ship, the interior of a mill, and a cavern filled with treasure, built for the film. When the producers hit a certain button on the control panel, the cavern set would flood!

In addition to shooting at the Disney studios, many of the large sets were built and sequences filmed in Wallilabou, Jamaica. The crew gradually transformed the town into the city of Port Royal, Jamaica in the 1600s. After the British Admiral Penn and General Venables captured Port Royal from the Spanish in 1654, the town became popular with pirates, who used it as a hangout where they could drink and sometimes even hide their treasure. Wallilabou was the perfect place for shooting because of its history and its similarity to Port Royal. Although Wallilabou Bay was the main location for the movie, some scenes were shot at Ottley Hall, Byahaut, and the Tobago Cays—all in Jamaica.

One near disaster stopped the filming briefly: One of the sets at Burbank Studios caught on fire. Producers and directors were terrified that some of their expensive sets would get ruined, or worse, their actors would get hurt. Thankfully, the fire was not devastating and there were only minimal damages. No one was hurt. The cast resumed filming almost immediately.

Will Turner, Orlando's character in *Pirates of the Caribbean*, is a young orphan who lives in Port Royal. He is an apprentice to the blacksmith, but is really more skilled than his boss. Because his boss is lazy and spends his time drinking or sleeping, Will takes on most of the duties in the shop, and through them learns a lot of responsibility and self-reliance.

Fun Fact:
In *Pirates of the Caribbean*, Orlando was the only cast member who did not wear a wig; he wore hair extensions instead.

As a tradesman, he is considered to be part of the lower class of society, but he is kind-hearted, honorable, and a true gentleman. He is in love with the wealthy and noble Elizabeth Swann, the governor's daughter and a childhood friend. Will was the only survivor on a ship that was completely destroyed by a pirate ship called the *Black Pearl*. He met Elizabeth for the first time when a ship on which she was sailing with her father rescued Will at sea. Will hates pirates because they killed his parents and burned the ship they were on. When he finds out that the father he never knew was actually a pirate—his mother told Will he was a sailor—he must reevaluate his views.

When Elizabeth is captured by Captain Barbossa of the *Black Pearl*, Will must put aside any lingering differences with the pirates and work with Captain Jack Sparrow, a pirate played by Johnny Depp, to rescue her. Finally Will is reunited with his love. However, he doesn't trust Jack Sparrow right away, and the two get into a few duels before finally becoming allies. Although Governor Swann had wished that his daughter would marry the nobleman Commodore Norrington, he eventually accepts Will and knows that he is the love of his daughter's life, even if he is a blacksmith and a pirate.

Orlando's role demanded that he prepare for several swordfighting scenes, many against Johnny Depp. The swordfighting he had to do was much more difficult than the bow and arrow work he did for the *Lord of the Rings* films. It required many more moves and more extensive fighting skills. He had to become quicker and more focused, because his moves had to be fast and sharp. He took fencing lessons with Bob Anderson, who trained the famous actor Errol Flynn. (In the pirate adventure *The Master of Ballantrae*, Bob was Errol's stunt double.)

Orlando's *Lord of the Rings* experience did leave him with a good idea of how fight scenes are shot. For fight scenes, actors constantly have to pause, shooting sequence by sequence to make sure that all of the moves are right and look natural.

The role of Will Turner again put Orlando in some adventurous and dangerous spots. In one scene he was rigged to the sails as he moved

Pre-Legolas, and so handsome

On location
for *The
Calcium Kid*

A "Dr Evil"
impression?

Heathrow Hunk—on his way to New York
from London

With girlfriend Kate Bosworth and
Aisha Tyler

Chris Weeks/WireImage

One of *GQ*'s
"Men of the
Year"

Mark Mainz/Getty Images

Elijah Wood, Dominic Monaghan, Orlando
and Billy Boyd

Meeting his fans

Butting heads with Viggo

Kevin Winter/Getty Images

A flash for the fans

Dean Treml/AFP/Getty Images

Gorgeous on *The Tonight Show with Jay Leno*

Kevin Winter/Getty Images

With fellow hottie
Mark Wahlberg

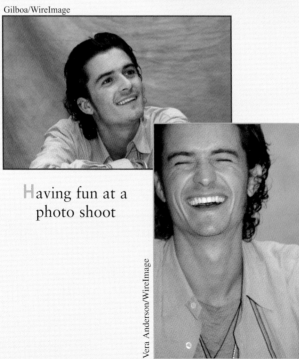

Having fun at a
photo shoot

Putting his best face forward

Fun Fact:
When Jack sprays Will's face with the sack of red powder in the blacksmith's shop, he is actually spraying him with powdered chocolate.

around the ship's set, so he would not get hurt. Orlando did many of the action shots and fighting scenes without the help of a stunt double. (He prefers not to use a stunt double unless really necessary.) In another scene, Orlando had to scream from the edge of the ship "I am Captain Will Turner!" The ship's deck and rails were wet and he was standing right on the edge. He could have fallen at any minute. The balance he gained from playing Legolas must have helped him keep his footing!

During filming, Johnny Depp became a close friend and role model to Orlando. Orlando was amazed by the way Johnny brought the character of Jack Sparrow to life on the screen. Johnny modeled the character on the attitude and voice of guitarist Keith Richards from The Rolling

Stones, so he had a very cool, sometimes silly way about him. Orlando has said that the script portrayed Johnny as a regular pirate, but Johnny brought much more to the role and made his character a larger-than-life, hilarious pirate whom everyone would remember.

Orlando has said that it is Johnny's amazing acting that has brought Johnny the recognition he has received over the years, in addition to his heartthrob good looks. He hopes he can achieve some of the same recognition that Johnny has gained.

In the summer of 2003, *Pirates of the Caribbean* was released into theaters and it soon became the blockbuster hit of the summer. It

Fun Fact:
Orlando often imitated Johnny's role in the movie, making everyone laugh. One day, while they were on a plane traveling to one of their film locations, Orlando did a hilarious impersonation of the star and Johnny and the producers loved it so much that they had it written into the script!

COOL QUOTES:

"It was a lot harder. There are a lot more moves. There's a lot more to learn. That was a huge sequence, particularly that opening sequence. I was quite intimidated by the whole idea of having to do that."
—Orlando on whether swordfighting was harder than archery, About.com

---

earned over $300 million in the United States, and $650 million around the globe. Because the movie was so successful, Disney has decided to make two sequels, and Orlando and Johnny have already signed up for both.

Orlando's honorable character, Will Turner, was a crowd favorite, and since Orlando was sporting his natural hair color in the movie instead of a long blond wig, he was suddenly noticed everywhere he went. Despite his popularity after the *Lord of the Rings* trilogy, it was still easy for him to walk the streets unnoticed since everyone knew him as Legolas. But now, everyone knew what the real Orlando looked like and he couldn't escape the public attention.

Orlando often asked Johnny Depp for advice on how to handle the screaming fans and sudden fame. Johnny's advice? Be gracious, be polite, and don't forget that these people put you where you are today.

After filming the movie, people noticed that he was wearing a pirate-like necklace in many of his pictures. Whether he was referring to a physical memento of a character, like a necklace, or something more spiritual when he said "The beautiful thing about being an actor is every character you embrace, when you move on, you take part of the character with you," Orlando definitely carries a piece of Will Turner with him.

Pirates of the Caribbean II is set to be released in 2005 or in the beginning of 2006. In an interview, Orlando revealed some secrets about the plot. In the beginning, everyone is preparing for the wedding of Will and Elizabeth Swann. However, right before the wedding, Elizabeth is kidnapped. Everyone thinks the culprit is Jack

---

PIRATE VOCABULARY:

Buccaneer: A pirate adventurer. A person who steals goods at sea, or land from the sea

Mariner: One who helps in steering and navigating a ship

Merchant ship: A ship that is involved in trade; a cargo ship

Vessel: Another name for a large ship

Booty: Goods obtained illegally; plunder taken from enemies after defeating them in battle

---

Sparrow, but Will knows better, and he begins to hunt for his beautiful fiancée.

His search leads him to the small island where Jack Sparrow is held hostage. Orlando's character has to defeat a one-eyed monster to save Jack, and together the two men continue the search for Elizabeth. Eventually we find out that a woman is behind the plot—Bermuda Barbossa, a daughter of the villian in *Pirates of the Caribbean: The Curse of the Black Pearl.*

She has kidnapped Elizabeth to get revenge on Will and Jack for her father's death.

The movie climaxes with a huge sea battle. One of the ships involved is the *Black Pearl II*.

CHAPTER FOUR

Making an Epic

"Amidst this epic, fantastic, huge sort of drama . . . it's very human at the crux of it. It deals with very human issues: anger, hate, love, fear, and all those things that lead a man to war, lead a country to war."
—Orlando Bloom describing the story of the Trojan War, *Premiere* magazine, May 2004

So what do you do after you've been a pirate, an outlaw, an elf, and a boxer? You become the famous prince of Troy, of course! Orlando's next role after *Pirates of the Caribbean* was playing Paris in *Troy*, a film based on the story of the legendary Trojan War. Directed by Wolfgang Peterson, the movie stars Brad Pitt as Achilles, Diane Kruger as Helen, and Eric Bana as Prince Hector. Orlando was excited to be a part of this huge project and its awesome cast, even though he was again leaving England—not for New Zealand this time, but for the beautiful coast of Malta.

> **Fun Fact:**
> Malta, where much of the filming for Troy took place, is an island in the Mediterranean. It is often called the "Heart of the Mediterranean" because it lies almost exactly in the middle of the sea.

Troy's producers had been having a hard time figuring out who to cast as Paris, but when they saw Orlando in the *Lord of the Rings* films and in *Black Hawk Down,* they organized a meeting with him right away. They were impressed by how intelligent and articulate he was. He also seemed to know the part of Paris well, and to understand why Paris did the things he did. Like Paris, Orlando is a very passionate and intense man. He has the features and body of a Trojan warrior, but the face of a passionate lover, just like Paris did. Knowing he would play Paris perfectly, the producers called Orlando the day after his audition to tell him that he had landed the role of the famous prince. As they worked out who would play the other roles, Orlando prepared for his part, again catching up on his reading.

Homer, a Greek poet, wrote *The Iliad* and *The Odyssey* around 800 BC. Both epic poems capture some of the foundational stories of Greek mythology. *The Iliad* centers on the Trojan War and *The Odyssey* continues the story of Odysseus after the end of the war. Orlando had always been interested in Greek mythology, so he enjoyed reading *The Iliad*; he also learned more about the complex character he would play.

Most of the film was shot in Malta, part of a group of islands about halfway between the coasts of Sicily and North Africa. Various Maltese locations were used, including Fort Ricasoli, Hal Far, Ghajn Tuffieha, Golden Bay, and Dwejra. Among the realistic sets constructed for the film were the majestic palace of Priam and the legendary forty-foot high Trojan horse, which included trapdoors on all sides for the

Fun Fact:

The Greeks believed in many gods, and their mythology is the stories behind the gods and goddesses. Each god or goddess had a special power or gift, and the stories in Greek mythology tell the stories of Greek history and morality. Often, the gods and humans would get themselves in all sorts of crazy situations. The Greek myths played out like a soap opera, filled with love, passion, sin, war, and murder. The priests at the time of the Trojan War were well educated on the myths of the gods and goddesses, and many people studied them because they were so interesting.

soldiers to come out of. The film helped the economy of Malta greatly, making it a more popular tourist spot; almost five hundred Maltese locals also worked on the set, and many had small parts in the film.

After leaving Malta, the cast and crew were supposed to continue filming at their next location in Morocco, but because of the war in Iraq, producers were worried about the safety of the cast and crew in what could have been a dangerous location. They chose to film in Mexico instead, so the crew had to move massive props—such as the Trojan horse—to Cabo San Lucas, Mexico.

Because of its beautiful weather and sandy beaches, Cabo San Lucas has become a huge tourist attraction over the years. This made producers nervous, seeing as they had high-profile celebrities like Orlando and Brad Pitt on the set. They feared that large crowds of sightseers and fans would not only distract the cast and crew and delay the film, but that they would ruin the secrets of the set for moviegoers later. In the end, the producers were able to keep the set closed to the public and filming continued.

> ### Fun Fact:
> Orlando and his fellow *Troy* cast members enjoyed filming in Cabo San Lucas, Mexico, partly because they got to enjoy the beautiful beaches and catch up on their tans between scenes.

The movie was very expensive to shoot. It cost $700,000 a day! Including the large salaries of the actors, the special effects, and the gigantic sets, the movie's budget came to about $200 million.

Orlando's character in *Troy* is Paris, a mortal. (Some of the characters in the film, as in the Greek myths themselves, are gods.) Paris is the son of King Priam and is known to be an honest and noble man. Although he is more of a lover than a fighter, his love for one woman would eventually cause the Trojan War.

Sparta, a kingdom under the rule of King Menelaus, and Troy are set to sign a treaty to allow free trade. Paris—Orlando's character— and his brother, Hector, are sent to Sparta to finish the treaty. When they arrive, Paris meets Helen, Menelaus's wife, and is immediately captivated by her great beauty. Knowing that he must have her, he forms a plan to bring her back to Troy with him. What had started as a peaceful mission was to escalate into an ugly war, putting many lives at risk.

Helen, who is unhappy in her marriage with Menelaus, falls in love with Paris, too, and goes along with Paris's plan to "kidnap" her and take

> ### COOL QUOTES:
>
> "Paris is a young man, and I'm a young man. And as a young man, you're coming to terms with an awful lot that you battle with. It's the seven deadly sins, you know, everyone's trying to understand what they mean to him. And so it's been a challenge . . . but a really exciting one!"
> —Orlando, on playing Paris,
> *Premiere* magazine, May 2004

her back to Troy. Helen waits patiently below the deck of Paris's ship while it sails away from her homeland. When they are safely at sea, Paris reveals to his brother Hector what he has done. Knowing that if he takes Helen back to Sparta his brother will be killed for kidnapping the queen, Hector reluctantly allows Paris and Helen to continue on to Troy.

When Paris returns with Helen, he is greeted with open arms. Although Paris's father, King Priam, is aware of the consequences of his son's actions, and realizes that the country might be on the brink of war, he lets Helen stay to please his son. Troy now has to suffer the consequences.

When King Menelaus discovers what has happened, he becomes extremely angry and goes to war against Troy in order to win back Helen. Agamemnon, his brother, goes with him. As the Greek army draws closer and closer to Troy, Paris is called to fight in the war. In a huge battle at the gates of Troy, Paris challenges King Menelaus to single combat. Although Paris survives the fight, he will have to fight many more battles to be with the woman he loves.

In one scene in the film, when Hector, Paris's brother, goes off to war, Paris feels regret for what he has done to Troy and to his family. He realizes that he has put many lives at stake. The Greek warrior Achilles (played by Brad Pitt in the movie) slays Hector and Paris avenges his brother's death by shooting Achilles in the tendon of his heel. This is the only vulnerable spot on the armor-clad warrior and he is killed.

Achilles is a very dark role; he's not a very happy guy. Brad Pitt wasn't even sure if he could pull off the role of Achilles at first, but before filming he prepared mentally and physically so

> **Fun Fact:**
> The phrase "Achilles' heel," meaning a person's vulnerable spot, comes from the fact that Achilles can only be brought down by shooting him in the tendon of his heel. It is his only weak spot.

that he could perform the part well. Brad even stopped smoking for his role! Paris is more of an archer, so all Orlando's training with bows and arrows in the *Lord of the Rings* films really came in useful! Orlando was very nervous about the scene where he shoots Achilles in the heel, because it meant shooting an actor he admired very much. Although he was used to dramatic battles and fight scenes by this time, Orlando was nervous working with such well-known actors on such a big film.

Not all of the fighting scenes were done by the actors themselves. For some of the spear and sword strikes, the actors used telescoping blades and spear points; in other scenes, they mimed thrusts, leaving the gore to be filled in later using computer graphics. In fact, computer graphics played a large role in creating Troy's realistic special effects. In order to create a battle scene with fifty thousand Greek soldiers charging at Hector, directors used five hundred extras and later multiplied the soldiers with computer graphics software written specifically for the film. By blending together the motions of the real soldiers, the graphics team could create animated soldiers with their own sets of actions and movements.

Makeup teams worked for hours creating wounds and scars—and boy did they look real! Producers wanted to make this film so that

---

COOL QUOTES:

"Brad is a great actor who becomes absorbed in his role so that he becomes his character. It impresses me that he doesn't only play the typical heroes."

—Orlando on working with Brad Pitt,
Moviestar magazine, October 2003

---

viewers would feel as if they were really there in ancient Troy. Orlando and Brad both wore costumes with huge pieces of armor, as well as tunics for scenes that did not involve battles. They wore their hair a little shorter than shoulder length, which was the typical style for men at that time. The women, such as Diane Kruger who plays Helen, also wore tunics, but theirs were different from the men's, as they would have been at the time.

Eric Bana plays Prince Hector, Orlando's character's brother. In addition to playing brothers on screen, Orlando and Eric became close friends behind the cameras. Eric has said that since filming *Troy,* he regards Orlando as "a real brother." And Orlando said that Eric is to him what "Hector is to Paris, a real rock." As soon as they met, they talked excitedly about the parts they were going to play. Bana also rides horseback, so often the two would go horseback riding to relieve some of the stress of filming.

Orlando also got along well with Brad Pitt, who was playing Achilles. He listened to Brad's advice on how to handle fame. Brad is well accustomed to the mobs of screaming and crying girls that follow celebrities, but for Orlando, it was a completely new experience. One day, while filming in Malta, Orlando and Brad decided to go out to some clubs. When they opened the door of the hotel lobby they saw crowds of fans holding signs and screaming their names. It must have been extremely flattering, but also a little unsettling.

Due to their high profiles, the stars of *Troy* often found it hard to go out or leave the set. Keeping a low profile, even in the secluded locations of Malta and Mexico, was difficult. But they managed to get out sometimes. Orlando and Brad were often spotted at Las Ventanas al Paraiso's al fresco Tequila & Ceviche Bar in Cabo San Lucas, a favorite among all the cast. The cast also went to the three-day Cabo Jazz Festival at the Pueblo Bonito Hotel and to the Sunset Beach Resort to hear performers including Chaka Khan and Nestor Torres.

When the filming was over, the cast-mates

were sad to leave their experience behind, but it would take quite a while before they saw the film they had worked so hard on. As with the *Lord of the Rings* movies, after all of the scenes were filmed, each one had to be edited and the special effects added to make sure everything looked realistic. The film was released in May 2004.

Orlando didn't waste any time after he finished *Troy.* He signed up to take on three more projects in 2004. Orlando is definitely a dedicated actor, and once he finds a role that fits him, he grabs it and excitedly embraces what's coming next!

CHAPTER FIVE

Orlando: Ladies' Man
or Hopeless Romantic?

"Women are beautiful. They deserve to be cherished and respected. . . . When you start falling for someone and you can't stop thinking about when you're going to see them again, I love that."

—Orlando Bloom on love, *Teen People*, 2003

If you were to ask Orlando Bloom about his love life, most likely silence would be his answer. Orlando is extremely private about who he's dating and in fact keeps most of his personal life separate from the media frenzy of his public life. He has said that you need to build a ten-meter-high wall around your heart and that celebrities are required to share their work with their fans, but not their personal lives.

Whether locking lips with hotties Keira Knightley or Diane Kruger on screen, or bouncing around town with movie superstars

Christina Ricci or Kate Bosworth, Orlando Bloom maintains the air of a man of mystery, at least in his love life. Nevertheless, Orlando would really like to meet someone special with whom he could connect.

It was rumored that Orlando was engaged to model-turned-makeup-artist Jemma Kidd, but due to their busy schedules and different lifestyles, the two supposedly split as Orlando was starting to film the *Lord of the Rings* trilogy. Orlando was also linked to actress Joanne Morley, who has said that the two still remain friends, even after the breakup.

COOL QUOTES:

"People come into your life and people leave it. I have quite a philosophical view on it. Certain things happen for a reason. You just have to trust that life has a road mapped out for you."

—Orlando in an interview
for *Company* (UK), April 2004

What other Hollywood starlets is Orlando rumored to have dated? In 2001, he was supposedly dating British actress Sienna Miller, who starred in the widely-anticipated British film *Polo*. Currently, Sienna is dating British heartthrob Jude Law. Then, in March 2002, Orlando was linked to actress Amy Smart, a blonde bombshell with several movie credits to her name, including *The Awful Truth*. It is also rumored that Orlando had a little bit of a fling with Maddy Ford, one of his cast-mates in *The Calcium Kid*. They supposedly spent some quality time together after the movie's wrap party at the Q bar in London. However, things ended quickly when Maddy had to leave to film in Los Angeles.

These days Orlando is not saying a word about the rumors surrounding his romantic rendezvous, leaving it to his fans to decide what to believe and trusting his family and friends to know the truth. However, Orlando is not afraid to scream from the highest mountain that he loves women in general. Growing up with his mom and sister, he has acquired a great appreciation for the beauty and compassion of females. He believes that women should be cherished, and he loves the spiral and adventure of falling in love. He is known to go out of his way for the women he loves. In one instance Orlando flew to Dubai, which is on the Persian Gulf, in order to spend time with someone he was pursuing. He also sent a girl a plane ticket to come visit him while he was filming, and he says he was lucky that she came.

COOL QUOTES:

"I do get to snog Orlando, yes. I'm rather smug about it actually. I'm quite worried I'm going to get lynched by teenage girls but to all teenagers out there: 'I'm really sorry and he's a great kisser!'"
—Keira Knightly in an interview for CBBC, August 2003

Although Orlando will not spill the beans on his love life, he does occasionally tell interviewers about his qualities as a boyfriend. He has admitted that he can become very close to the girls he dates and that he tries to make every

date a fun and exciting one. He considers himself fun, and very "full-on," when he's dating
someone, but overall extremely easygoing. He
is the kind of guy you can joke around with,
have a good time with, and be just plain silly
with whenever you want.

One aspect of his love life Orlando has
revealed is that he had his first kiss when he was
twelve years old. He said that it was a complete
and total disaster! He had no idea what to do
with his teeth, and to this day he gets embarrassed when he thinks about it. He's had more
practice now and his co-stars admit that
Orlando is a very good kisser.

When looking for a woman, Orlando concen-
trates on what she is after. Is she going to date
him just for his looks, fame, or friends? Or is
she going to love him because he is himself, and
a name means nothing? In Hollywood, he
knows you have to be careful who you date
because people can fall in love with an image or
a name, with no idea what the real person is
like. Orlando does not want to be part of "just

another Hollywood couple" and thinks that high-profile relationships are often a disaster. The best way to maintain a good romance, according to Orlando: Keep your lips sealed!

COOL QUOTES:

"Women expect a blonde god, because of Legolas, but it is a wig. In real life my hair is short. And I'm happy with that, because people don't recognize me very much. I can walk in the streets peacefully."

—Orlando in an interview for *Hitkrant* magazine, 2003

Quiet about his private life to the press and in interviews, Orlando Bloom nevertheless does confide in his friends and family, telling his close friends everything, and then asking them not to share his secrets. Some have talked about spending nights at bars with Orlando, checking out cute girls. Orlando is often seen out on the town with the "hobbits" from the *Lord of the Rings* cast, Elijah Wood, Sean Astin, Dominic Monaghan, and Billy Boyd.

Occasionally Orlando will comment on his

private life if he feels the newspapers and magazines have gotten it really wrong. When rumored to be seeing *Casper* cutie Christina Ricci, Orlando put his foot down and told the fans and the newspapers that this is absolutely not true. Ricci and Orlando were seen dancing pretty closely together at a post-Oscar party in Los Angeles, California. They were also seen chatting at a few clubs. But Orlando says they are just friends.

Although Orlando tries his best to keep his personal life confidential, a picture is worth a thousand words. Recently, Bloom has been photographed with actress Kate Bosworth. Kate is the star of *Blue Crush*, in which she plays a surfer battling to make a mark on the professional surfing world and hopefully finding love along the way. Orlando and Kate have been seen dining and dancing around town, and Orlando confirmed they have a relationship in an interview in December 2003.

The duo has been seen in the Burbank airport in Los Angeles, which was one of their more public sightings. Kate was waiting patiently for the *Lord of the Rings* star to come off a flight. As he walked out of the corridor the two locked eyes and Kate jumped into Orlando's arms. He picked her up and swung her in circles, looking ecstatic to see his supposed flame. Apparently, the two are somewhat serious, and Orlando is looking for a house in Los Angeles that they can share. Last Christmas, Kate spent the week with Orlando in his current home in Los Angeles. It was also reported that Orlando bought Kate a very expensive bracelet, which he gave to her while they were out to dinner with some friends. Orlando admits that Kate is a great girl.

"Orlando likes to keep tight-lipped about his personal life but he's made no secret of the fact that he's smitten with Kate. You just have to see them together to realize what a good team they make. Most couples would struggle given the fact that Kate is based in Los Angeles and Orlando in London, but they both just know its right."
—Reported by the British *Daily Star* in February 2004

Even though the happy couple wishes to keep their love life a secret, the newspapers, television reporters, and tabloid writers have been searching high and low for any evidence of the relationship they can find. A British tabloid reported this year that Orlando was going to propose to Kate, and that he admitted this. But there has been no confirmation of that. And if Orlando has his way—with his private nature, if he was going to propose, you can be sure that the tabloids would be the last to hear about it.

So what does Orlando look for in a girl? He prefers nice, sweet girls who aren't afraid to do all of the fun, adventurous things that he loves. He says that he is a sucker for blond girls with outgoing personalities. He has said he likes average, down-to-earth girls.

Fun Fact:

According to *People* magazine ("50 Most Beautiful People" Issue, April 2004), Orlando's nose is one of the most often requested by people having plastic surgery!

How Compatible Are You with Orlando?

Orlando was born in January, which makes him a Capricorn. Capricorns are loving, devoted and intense boyfriends. They are responsible, goal-oriented, and career-focused. Match Orlando's sign up with your birth sign to see if you would be the ideal girlfriend for Orlando.

ARIES:

If you are an Aries, you are probably the life of the party. You are loud and flashy and like to be seen. Capricorn is more reserved, so you can expect some clashes of opinions. If you want to stay together, you will have to agree to disagree. You can teach one another things you wouldn't learn on your own.

TAURUS:

Taurus and Capricorn are both very sensible and share a down-to-earth nature. Capricorn will push Taurus to reach her goals, and together this couple can accomplish many things. But watch out—all work and no play is never any fun!

GEMINI:

Capricorn and Gemini are very different so they need to make time for some compromise if they want their love to last. Capricorn has to give Gemini the room to be creative, and Gemini needs to realize that in order to maintain balance, Capricorn needs focus and hard work.

CANCER:

Cancer brings a charge of emotional intensity to the relationship, while Capricorn balances it. Both hold each other to high standards. In a Capricorn, Cancer finds dedication, and in return Capricorn comes to love Cancer's determination. These two signs can come together to create a very successful and secure connection.

LEO:

Leo and Capricorn both love to be the center of attention and material possessions are important to them. Leo can be outrageous, while Capricorn is more old-fashioned, of a more simple nature. Because both signs are so strong-minded, with a bit of attention they will sympathize with one another. Leo and Capricorn have a lot to learn from each other.

VIRGO:

Virgo can help Capricorn to relax a little and be grateful for all he has worked to accomplish. Capricorn can help Virgo reach her goals and make her dreams a reality. They live a very comfortable life together.

LIBRA:

Not a perfect love match, but can work with patience and understanding. Capricorn must try not to discourage Libra from her natural passion and confidence, and Libra must do her best to help Capricorn remain balanced.

SCORPIO:

Possibly one of the best love matches for Capricorn. From Scorpio, Capricorn will learn the value of looking below the surface of things, the rich pleasure that can come from deeply knowing another person. Both signs share a love of dedication. If they decide a relationship is their next big goal to achieve, there's no stopping these two.

SAGITTARIUS:

Sagittarius can show Capricorn adventure and thrill. Capricorn teaches Sagittarius to control her random energy, to pay attention to detail, and to discover that the little things are important. Sagittarius may view Capricorn as too responsible, and will teach her partner to lighten up.

CAPRICORN:

When it comes to maintaining a healthy relationship, this couple can really take care of business, so much so that they will have to be extra careful not to spend too much time working and not enough time having fun. Reliable and giving, this couple is loving and devoted without being over-bearing, which is a pleasing mixture for each partner.

AQUARIUS:

Capricorn will show Aquarius a life based on organization, rationality, and comfort. Capricorn has a more careful, ratio-nal outlook on life, while Aquarius is insatiable, nurturing an unrealistic approach to everything. They may seem like total opposites, but once these two set eyes on each other, a per-manent bond is formed.

PISCES:

This couple is honest, and can be devoted to each other. They admire each other: Capricorn likes Pisces's kind nature, and Pisces is drawn in by Capricorn's quick humor and per-sistence. The Capricorn—Pisces duo can really put their heads together and can be happy in their relationship.

CHAPTER SIX

What's Next for Orlando?

"I know you can be up one minute and drop the next, so I'm trying to maintain a steady course so I can have some longevity."

—Orlando on being an actor, *Harper's Bazaar* (Singapore), February 2002

Orlando continues to find success with his movies. The audiences love him, the girls adore him, and the directors can't wait to get their hands on him. Everything has been going just the way he must have imagined it would when he walked the halls of his London school and saw the photo of Ewan McGregor. Orlando couldn't wait to jump into more projects when he finished filming *Troy*, and he has many great things ahead of him.

After Orlando completed *Troy*, he decided to take on a character that he was well acquainted with—a British wild child. The movie, titled *Haven,* is directed by Frank E. Flowers. The story follows two shady conmen, played by Bill Paxton and Gabriel Byrne, who lead Orlando's character into a life of crime. Orlando also decided to take the next step and not only act in *Haven,* but also co-produce the movie.

Fun Fact:
Haven was director Frank E. Flowers' first film!

Haven takes place over one weekend as two shady businessmen make their escape to the Cayman Islands. They are trying to avoid prosecution by the federal government. Their flight sets off a series of events that eventually involve Orlando's character, Shy, in a crime. The movie was filmed on location in the Cayman Islands in the Caribbean, roughly halfway between Cuba and the Central American country of Honduras.

Once again, Orlando was filming on sunny beaches amid posh restaurants and fancy resorts. This time, though, it was a smaller set than the large, extravagant sets of *Troy* or the *Lord of the Rings* trilogy.

The movie doesn't have a firm release date yet, but people are already talking about it. Star Bill Paxton gave an interview to *Cinematic*

Do you want to know all of the latest info on Orlando's movies? Here is a list of websites all about Orlando and his films:

The official *Lord of the Rings* website:
http://www.lordoftherings.net

The official *Lord of the Rings* fan club:
http://www.lotrfanclub.com

The official *Pirates of the Caribbean* website:
http://www.pirates.movies.com

The official *Ned Kelly* website:
http://www.nedkellythemovie.com

The official *Black Hawk Down* website:
http://www.sonypictures.com/movies/blackhawkdown

The official *Troy* website:
http://www.troymovie.warnerbros.com

Happenings Under Development (chud.com) and said he felt *Haven* would be "the hot indie of the year." It is an independent film, which is another departure from the big-budget studio films Orlando has been doing. Another change: Orlando will not be swordfighting in this one!

Orlando has also been cast in the lead role of Ridley Scott's new movie, *Kingdom of Heaven*. Ridley worked with Orlando in *Black Hawk Down,* so he knows what a talented actor Orlando is. *Kingdom of Heaven* is an adventure with a healthy dose of romance. It is set during the Crusades and it's a much bigger movie than *Haven*—more like *Troy* or *Pirates of the Caribbean* with big stars and extensive sets. Orlando will also get to pick up his sword again as he battles Crusaders throughout the movie. He plays the role of Balian, a blacksmith turned knight who saves a kingdom and falls in love with the princess of Jerusalem while defending the city against the Crusaders.

Kingdom of Heaven began shooting in Spain in January of 2004, and Orlando was looking

> **Cool Fact:**
> Orlando played an apprentice to a blacksmith in *Pirates of the Caribbean* and will play a blacksmith who must fight as a knight in his upcoming film, *Kingdom of Heaven.*

forward to working with Ridley Scott again. From his experiences with *Black Hawk Down*, he knew Ridley Scott was a great director and that the film would be wonderful. Orlando says he likes to work with people he knows because it makes filming a lot less stressful. A friendly environment is more fun.

> **COOL QUOTES:**
> "I'm really grateful to Ridley for giving me the opportunity, but because also I know Ridley will make a great movie. Like I'm in the hands of a master. As long as I keep my end of the bargain, I know he's going to deliver, and I know I can kind of deliver so I hope it's going to come through. I think the star of that movie will be the way that he makes it. He's that kind of a guy, so I'm really glad that that was the first [lead role]."
> —Orlando on playing Balian, interview with Fred Toppel, 2004

So who is the lucky girl who gets to play Orlando's princess? Ridley Scott and the producers wanted to find the perfect girl. They searched and searched until they uncovered unknown actress Eva Green, who will be seen first in the Bernardo Bertolucci film *The Dreamers*. Eva is a French actress and although she is not yet well known in the United States, after the release of *Kingdom of Heaven* her name will most likely be all over the papers, much like Keira Knightley's popularity exploded after *Bend It Like Beckham* and *Pirates of the Caribbean* were released. Eva admitted that she is quite nervous about working with actors of Orlando's caliber, and with Orlando in particular because he is so well known and so handsome.

Even though Orlando had a very busy filming schedule, he still had time for his girlfriend Kate. She spent time with him in Spain, staying the whole month of February while Orlando was filming there.

Kingdom of Heaven is set to be released in

COOL QUOTES:

"The thing with Ridley [Scott] is he's been doing this forever, he knows what it is he wants and how to get it. . . . There's absolutely no messing around on set. Having said that, he's very accessible to actors, very open to what you want to do and willing to talk about it. He casts people who he feels are going to bring something to the role and allows them to take care of the situation, to do what it is that they do."

—Orlando on working with Ridley Scott, *Harper's Bazaar* (Singapore), February 2002

May 2005. Meanwhile, in July 2004, Orlando is set to begin filming *Elizabethtown,* a movie in which he plays a man named Drew Baylor. Baylor is on the verge of suicide after a shoe company where he works fires him. Then, right after he is fired, his girlfriend, Ellen, dumps him. He feels hopeless and alone, and if this wasn't enough, his father dies. Baylor must go back to his hometown of Elizabethtown for the funeral. On the way there, he meets flight attendant Claire Colburn, with whom he starts to fall in love. The two begin a romance that brings hope to Drew's life and encourages him to believe that there is a future, even after all the bad things that have just happened.

In this movie, Orlando is set to work with an all-star cast once again. Susan Sarandon will play Drew's mother, and Kirsten Dunst will be playing Claire, his love interest. Jessica Biel, from the WB's television show *Seventh Heaven* and the film *Summer Catch* (with Freddie Prinze, Jr.) is set to play his ex-girlfriend, Ellen, who has just cruelly dumped him when the film begins.

Unlike his previous roles and films, this one is set in the current time period and Orlando is finally playing a modern role. He has said that he often feels trapped in time because so many of his roles have taken place in the past. His role in *Elizabethtown* was originally set for Ashton Kutcher from MTV's *Punk'd* series and Fox's *That '70s Show.* Kutcher backed out and Orlando was next up for the role.

Orlando will also be filming the sequel to *Pirates of the Caribbean,* which is scheduled to be released in summer 2006. The movie is set to begin filming at the end of the summer (2004), and is tentatively titled *Pirates of the Caribbean II: The Treasure of the Lost Abyss*. Keira Knightley and Johnny Depp are both returning to their roles. Orlando will have to travel back in time once again, to play a pirate and wield a sword.

Fun Fact:

When Orlando was a little boy, he loved watching pirate movies on Saturday mornings. Then, he would go outside and imitate the moves that the pirates were doing in the movie. He would be the bad guy and Samantha would be the hero.

At twenty-seven years old, Orlando is clearly unstoppable. His dedication and hard work land him fantastic roles in the best locations, with the best co-stars! We'll be seeing him on the big screen for a long time to come.

Orlando's Film Roles:

Past and Current Films:

Troy

Pirates of the Caribbean

The Calcium Kid

Wilde

The Lord of the Rings trilogy

Ned Kelly

Black Hawk Down

Future Films:

The Journey Is the Destination

Elizabethtown

Kingdom of Heaven

Pirates of the Caribbean II

Haven

CHAPTER SEVEN

The Bloomatics

> "The girls have got a bit excited. I spoke to my agent and she says she's wading through the fan mail. We've got bags of it."
> —Orlando on his fans, *Express on Sunday* (UK), 2002

Are you constantly looking up the latest news on Orlando? Do you sigh when you see one of the many beautiful pictures of him that circulate on the Internet? Do you secretly (or not so secretly) hate his current girlfriend, Kate Bosworth, for "stealing your man"? Well, if any of these things sounds like you, you have fallen victim to Orlandomania! But don't think you are alone; there are millions of "Bloomatics" all across the globe, and they all share the same exact thing: a genuine love and admiration for the wonderfulness that is Orlando! They range from little girls to old women; they speak the languages of over twenty countries; they come from all backgrounds and walks of life; but they all know that Orlando is the best actor they have ever seen.

Orlando Bloom has become a household name—and who can he thank other than his adoring fans? Not only have Orlando's fans transformed the once-unknown actor into a well-known "teen idol," but he has also developed something of a cult following. Are they obsessed? Maybe, or maybe they just caught on to something everyone else will eventually embrace. Hundreds if not thousands of webpages have been lovingly dedicated to the beautiful Briton from Canterbury.

> **Fun Fact:**
> Orlando's famous nicknames "Orli" and "OB" were made up by his Internet fans!

Orlando has made quite a leap from minor characters such as a rent boy in *Wilde* to central characters such as Legolas in the *Lord of the Rings* trilogy. Along with this leap to starring roles came screaming fans. Even famous faces have admitted to being a fan of Orlando. Many of his co-stars praise his marvelous acting, including Sir Ian McKellen, who has said about Orlando, "Well it is a spectacular debut [in *The Fellowship of the Ring*], and he's got fans all over the world, quite rightly, as one of the fellowship" (Capital FM interview, 2002).

Orlando's other co-star Diane Kruger (who plays Helen alongside Orlando and Brad Pitt in the film *Troy*) has also noticed the level of stardom Orlando has reached: "When we started shooting, no one really knew who he was—he'd made *Lord of the Rings* but he looked so different in that. . . . Halfway through shooting *Troy*, *Pirates of the Caribbean* came out. It was pretty extraordinary to witness someone going from basically nothing to having girls screaming whenever we stepped out the door" (TeenHollywood.com, 2004). She must realize now just how lucky she was to kiss Mr. Bloom over and over again in *Troy*!

"Orlando is a movie star waiting to happen,"

Gregor Jordan, who directed him in *Ned Kelly*, said to Scotsman.com. "He's going to be huge because he's a good actor and he has incredible presence. There's a reason why girls go crazy for him. There's just something about him that makes people want to sit in the dark and watch him on the movie screen."

There definitely is something about Orlando, something that makes all of us go crazy when we hear his name or catch a glimpse of him on television. It must be a combination of his looks, his sweet attitude, and his down-to-earth nature that really draws us to him.

But the true fans are definitely the girls (and boys) running websites online. According to an interview with British talk show host, Graham Norton, in October 2003, Orlando has many, many websites dedicated to him (and he says his mom checks up on all of them), and the number keeps rising with Orlando's fame. Orlando humbly acknowledged his Internet fans when asked (during the promotion of *Lord of the Rings: The Return of the King*) whether he visited their websites: "I haven't. I haven't done any of that. I've been told an awful lot about it, and again, it's great that people. . . . I think the Internet is another thing that's relatively new to the world and they've picked up on different ways of doing things . . . and I happen to be one of them [laughs]."

The reason that Orlando never checks his fan sites is not because he doesn't want to see all of the great things written about him, but because he really hates computers! He has been quoted as saying that he thinks the Internet is "scary," and often "a little dangerous." Orlando doesn't watch much television either. His mother has been trying to convince him to get his own official website but Orlando has said that is not necessary, since his movies speak for themselves.

Online fans have become a force to be reckoned with in the Orlando Bloom media world. A fan's word is definitive in this world. On April 1, 2004, the website ka-bloom.org posted a news brief stating that Orlando had taken on a "new look." The website went on to explain that Orlando had gone bald for his latest film *Kingdom of Heaven*. While the story was obviously an April Fool's joke, a few days later *Greek TV Guide* printed the story as fact in its periodical!

As the *Greek TV Guide* story proves, Orlando Bloom fans are scattered across the globe. Fans come from places ranging from Orlando's homeland, England, to the United States, to Australia—and we cannot forget the masses of "Orli" fans in Japan.

So dedicated are Orlando's fans that they even started a huge scrapbook for the actor's twenty-sixth birthday. The scrapbook was eighty-eight pages long and its contributors ranged from twelve-year-old girls to women over fifty. Twenty-one states and twenty-two countries were represented in the huge Orlando Bloom birthday project. Fans sent photographs of themselves, their friends, their pets, their rooms, and their cities and countries. Some sent hand-drawn sketches, poetry, and graphic art. In addition to the scrapbook, fans donated over $2,000

Here are some of the most popular Orlando sites on the Web today. Check them out and find fans just like you!

Full Bloom
http://www.full-bloom.net

The Bloom Room
http://www.bloom-room.net

The Orlando Bloom Files
http://www.theorlandobloomfiles.com

Orlando Bloom Multimedia
http://www.orlandomultimedia.net

Orlando Bloom Central
http://www.orlandocentral.net

in his name to Greenpeace, an organization that Orlando supports.

The next year, the fan group did something very similar for Orlando's twenty-seventh birthday, donating more money to charity and putting even more time into creating something for his birthday that was truly unique and special. Orlando even replied to the kindness of his fans himself, thanking them for their extreme generosity!

Orlando loves getting sweet fan mail. He likes when girls notice more than just his looks. He wants people to like him for him, and not just for his pretty face, or for the characters he plays.

Even though Orlando has so many fans around the globe, the fame has not gone to his head. Orlando says, "I have an older sister, Samantha, who would never let that happen. I have a cousin who would never let that happen. And I've surrounded myself with friends who would beat me—physically—if for a moment I tried to get above myself" (*Dolly,* Australia, 2002).

Orlando's charm, down-to-earth nature, and mysteriousness are usually cited by his fans as their reason for admiring the actor (*ahem,* that *and* his good looks). Orlando has won many voter-based honors such as Hottest Male in

> *COOL QUOTES:*
>
> "If I imagine that some fans wait for five hours and sac-
> rifice an entire afternoon to see their star, I think it is
> right to take a bit of time to give autographs. I myself
> would never do that. You need to arrange yourself.
> Otherwise you only live in fear and you are no longer
> able to enjoy life. Something a friend once told me that
> has helped me: There will always be new young musicians
> or actors that are adored by teenagers. They do need it
> for their wishes, longings, fantasies, or whatsoever. This
> makes sense to me and ever since I see things a lot
> more relaxed."
>
> —Orlando on being idolized by girls,
> *Moviestar* (Germany), 2003

Total Film (UK) in March 2003, Most
Attractive Man of 2003 by *Hello!* magazine,
and Best Film Actor by *GQ* in 2003. He was
named one of *People* magazine's 50 Most
Beautiful People in its April 2004 issue. He also
has a record of winning many of *Hello!* magazine's weekly Most Attractive Man polls online.
And how does Orlando feel about his rise to

COOL QUOTES:

"I'm not the type who is worried about looks. Sometimes I don't shave for days simply because I don't feel like it. I also don't pay attention to my hair. I simply let it grow. To go to the barber is annoying and evil. But I'm in the lucky position to get a haircut during shootings."

—Orlando, when asked if he was vain,
Petra (Germany), 2003

fame? "I still sort of don't believe its all happening. It's surreal. The goal was to get paid as an actor. That would have been enough" (*GQ*, 2004). He says that he is not at all annoyed at the attention he's getting, but he would like to be known as a talented actor and not just as a sex symbol. He also doesn't want to be known as his characters, but rather for who he really is. He has said that his fans "are cool, they're sweet, but they just don't know me. They've just seen the characters I play. I'm flattered that they respond to them, but that's not me" (*Empire, UK*, 2003).

Orlando is constantly thankful, though, for

his fans, because he knows that they made him the superstar he is today. Without their support for his movies, he might not have the opportunities to play the roles he loves. Orlando tries to answer all of his fan mail, though it has become difficult with so many letters pouring in from all over the world. Orlando's correspondence team says that he receives over six hundred letters a week!

If you would like to write to Orlando, make sure you include a self-addressed, stamped envelope. If you do not live in the United States, you should include three international reply coupons, which you can find at your local post office. Send your letter to one of these two addresses:

Orlando Bloom
c/o Aleen Keshishian
The Firm
9100 Wilshire Blvd.
Suite 400 West
Beverly Hills, CA 90212
USA

Orlando Bloom
c/o Chris Andrews
ICM
8942 Wilshire Blvd.
Beverly Hills, CA
90211
USA

LOVIN' BLOOM

So you have his posters all over your wall? You talk about Orlando all the time? You even have your own website dedicated to Orlando? Well, you must be the biggest Orlando fan, right? WRONG. The self proclaimed number one Orlando fan is none other than Mrs. Bloom—Orlando's mom!

CELEBRITY FAN:
Lindsay Lohan, star of *Mean Girls*, declared Orlando the hotest guy on the scene in *People* magazine, April 2004. "He's gorgeous. . . . He does really great films and he sets himself aside from all the other actors."

CHAPTER EIGHT

Life Away From the Cameras

"I can be a little bit outrageous. I can be a lot of things. I'm a bit of an adrenaline junkie, so I love to go out there and do kind of crazy stuff which is slightly outrageous, like bungee jumping, skydiving, surfing and that sort of stuff. But I also like to just chill with my friends and go and see movies and do normal things."
—Orlando in an interview for the CBBC

So what does a big time celebrity do when he's not . . . umm . . . being a big-time celebrity? Well, Orlando is just like everyone else. He loves when his work is done so that he can have time to relax and hang out with the people he loves. His favorite place to be is London, and even though he spends a lot of time at his house in Los Angeles, he wouldn't give up England for the world. It is where he grew up, where he learned everything he knows, and where he has formed his most lasting friendships. He likes being home because he can be close to his mother, with whom he has a very close relationship. Orlando says that his mother is the most important woman in his life and he asks for her advice all of the time.

We know from Orlando's experiences while filming the *Lord of the Rings* trilogy that he is quite the daredevil. He loves extreme sports such as surfing and snowboarding, and has always wanted to learn how to skateboard. After trying it for the first time in New Zealand, Orlando has formed a new love for bungee jumping. He has said that the feeling before you jump is exhilarating. Since his near-death experience when he broke his back as a teenager, he has learned that life is truly worth living, and that a person who never takes risks never truly lives. He has no regrets about the daring stunts he has done.

When he isn't pulling his crazy stunts or hitting the beaches or the snow, Orlando is a bit of a homebody. He loves to hang out at home, and although he doesn't watch television, he does love watching movies. Since he rarely gets to relax, being able to sit down to watch movies with his friends or family is a great opportunity for Orlando to chill out.

Orlando also loves long walks on the beach. He has filmed on so many beachside locations that he has had many opportunities to enjoy the beach and find solace in the ocean. He says that the ocean and the sand help him ease whatever is on his mind.

Orlando has always been very creative, and he enjoys taking pictures as well as sculpting. Both have been a passion of his since he was in school. He tries to make time to sculpt when he can, and he often has his camera with him when he's traveling, or even just hanging out at home.

Orlando is an animal lover and an outspoken vegetarian. He doesn't drink milk, despite his role in *The Calcium Kid,* but he loves soy milk. The last time he ate meat was right after he injured his back as a teenager. Doctors told him that eating steak would help his back to heal quicker. He followed their orders and says that they must have been right, because his back healed much faster than expected.

He was very upset when he had to give away his beloved dog Maud because he was filming all the time. However, he gave Maud to a close friend, so he knows that his beloved pooch is in good hands. He recently bought a new puppy to take Maud's place.

Orlando also loves horses, and his experiences on the *Lord of the Rings* set have taught him to be a strong horseback rider. He has said that one day he would like to own horses because they are such beautiful creatures and he enjoys riding them so much.

Orlando also loves music, and tries to get out to concerts whenever he can.

So as you can see, even though Orlando is a big-time celebrity, he's just like all of us. He doesn't like to work all the time, and he loves to relax and be with those he cares about. He has hobbies and interests that he pursues in his private time. He hasn't adopted a glitzy Hollywood lifestyle, preferring to keep his life private. He wants to keep normalcy in his life—no matter how famous he becomes, he will still be the same guy from a small town outside London, who loves the simple things and needs his friends and family to keep him grounded.

SOME OF HIS FAVORITE THINGS . . .
AND HIS FIRSTS

Favorite Actors: Like many of us, Orlando admires
   veteran actors Daniel Day-Lewis, Johnny Depp,
   Paul Newman, and Edward Norton.

Favorite Color: Yellow

Favorite Foods: Italian rules! Orlando loves pasta
   and pizza. He also likes other starches such as
   oatmeal and rice and baked potatoes.

Favorite Movies: *Stand By Me, The Hustler*

Favorite Music: Songs by bands such as
   Radiohead, Coldplay, and U2. Orlando also likes
   singers such as Bob Dylan, Ben Harper, and David Gray.

Favorite Sports: Orlando loves snowboarding and
   surfing.

Favorite Team: Orlando roots for soccer team
   Manchester United. He is a David Beckham fan, so

now that Becks plays for Real Madrid, Orlando also roots for them.

Favorite Vegetable: To keep up his strength, like Popeye, Orlando loves to eat spinach.

First Car: A VW Golf—forest green.

First CD He Remembers Buying: Probably Edie Brickell and the New Bohemians. Michael Jackson's *Thriller* was probably the first record he bought, before CDs were available.

First Concert: Orlando's first concert was a Jamiroquai performance in his hometown of Canterbury, England.

First Crush on a Famous Person: Who didn't love Linda Evans on *Dynasty*?

First Movie Role: He played a rent boy in *Wilde*.